The Song o' Sorlomun

being

The Song of Solomon

translated into Norfolk dialect

by

Revd Edward Gillett

The Larks Press

First printed and published in this edition by
The Larks Press
Ordnance Farmhouse, Guist Bottom, Dereham.

November 1993

British Library Cataloguing-in-Publication Data.
A catalogue record for this book is available from the British Library,

ISBN 0 948400 21 8

The Song of Solomon
an Introduction by the Revd Richard Hale

Two books of the Bible have no religious content: 'Esther', which gained a place as part of the Jewish national epic, and the 'Song of Solomon', a collection of love poems which seems an odd intrusion. The inclusion of these poems in the recognised Scriptures owes much to the presumed authorship of Solomon. In the first book of Kings we read 'Solomon uttered three thousand proverbs and his songs were a thousand and five'. Since his name appears in some of the poems, later ages unhesitatingly attributed them to Solomon.

Modern scholars date them on linguistic grounds to the third century B.C., though they may contain earlier material and embody traditional love-songs. But how could such directly erotic poems find a place in the Scriptures? It was not easily won. Not until the Synod of Jumnia in 100 A.D. was the 'Song of Solomon' accepted as part of the Hebrew Canon, and even then with the significant proviso that it should only be read by men over thirty years old! A later curse on any who should recite it in wine shops shows continuing suspicion. Religious use could only be justified by allegorical treatment of the poems. The love they described became an allegory of God's love for his chosen people. Treated thus, they were deemed appropriate, reading for the Passover celebration of God's saving love for Israel.

There are no references to the 'Song of Solomon' in the New Testament, but when the Christian Church adopted the Hebrew scriptures as the Old Testament, it was included, but with a changed interpretation. It was now an allegory of the love of Christ for his bride, the Church, and as such afforded an ample field for the preacher. St. Bernard preached eighty-six sermons on the first two chapters alone! This allegorical interpretation is easily accessible in the chapter headings of the 1611 Authorised Version.

Chapter 1, 'The Church's love unto Christ: She confesseth her deformity: and prayeth to be directed to his flock: Christ directeth her to the shepherd's tent: the Church and Christ congratulate one another'. As the cult of the Virgin Mary developed, later medieval churchmen found new meanings in the 'Song of Solomon'. The Rose of Sharon, the Lilies, the garden enclosed became part of the Marian symbolism used by preachers and artists, and some poems found their way into the Liturgy. When we hear settings of 'I am black but comely' or 'Thou art fair my love' in Monteverdi's 'Vespers', we remember that these are the Vespers of the Blessed Virgin Mary'.

In later times allegorical interpretation was ridiculed. Horace Walpole in a letter remarks that 'if the Bride is the Church, the vineyard must be the churchyard'. The poems of the 'Song of Solomon' are now accepted for what they are — a celebration of Love, and Scripture is enriched by the inclusion of this expression of the love of man and woman which is one of the greatest graces of human life. The 1611 translation is felicitous and has proved very memorable. 'For lo, the winter is past, the rain is over and gone. The flowers appear on the earth, the time of the singing of birds is come.' 'Until the day breaks, the shadows flee away.'

That the 'Song of Solomon' was widely known to some is shown by a pleasant love letter from a dubiously literate young man to his beloved, picked up in 1887 on Sidmouth beach. He addresses his Mary throughout in the same way as he finishes:

'Dearest Marey, pure and holy and meek and lowly rose of Sharon, I be very appy to say our old Sow As got 7 yung uns and Father is going to gi us a roosester for our Weding Brakefast. Deerest Marey pure and holey meek and loly Rose of Sharon from your fewture loving husband

William Taylor.'

William would have liked the translation of the Revd Edward Gillett!

Notes on the Norfolk Dialect
by the Revd Edward Gillett

The dialect spoken in Norfolk and Suffolk differs from English more in pronunciation than in any other respect. As no phonetic spelling with which I am acquainted can fairly render the Norfolk 'drant' or the Suffolk 'whine', I have not attempted it. The Suffolk 'whine' is a more drawling intonation than the 'drant' There is a common tendency to silabate words by prefixing 's,' as squench for quench (vii. 7), stroam for roam (iii. 2), &c.

The pronouns thou, thee &c. are almost entirely disused, being only retained in some salutations. 'Far' thĕ well.' 'Sam' onto thee,' the constant response to the toast, 'Here's t'ye!' This, as Mr. Spurdens acutely discovered, is the mysterious word 'Sammodithee,' so long the torment of Norfolk philologists.

'Be,' however, is used as the present tense of the verb in all persons, principally in the phrases, 'Here I be;' 'Here ye be!' 'Here t' be' (here it is), &c.

You, your, are pronounced yow, yĕ, yar, yer, according as they require emphasis or not. 'Together' is used as a pronoun of multitude, always in the vocative; 'Here's a nice harvest day, together!' would be a salutation to a company of mowers. Indeed, it has been wittily observed that in Norfolk 'Together' is the plural of 'Bor.'

We retain the power of altering the intensity of meaning of a word, whether verb, adjective, or substantive, by altering the vowel; and use this power with almost all monosyllables, as well as many other words. Thus, in addition to the English forms drip, drop, droop, we have 'dreep' and 'drōpe'; the former an intensitive of drip, the latter of drop, as viscous liquids, - tar, honey, melted tallow, &c. (IV., 11; V. 5).

We have many preterites also formed by changing the vowel, in addition to those in classic English; 'Hew', did hoe; 'sew' (pronounced sew) did sew, &c. Thus hewd, heuld, hild, are all preterites of hold; wove, rōve, dōve, of wave, rive, dive, the latter word always being pronounced deeve. Singularly enough, this last word is considered correct in America, and is used by Longfellow, canto vi.:—

> 'Straight into the river, Kwasind
> Plunged as if he were a beaver
> Dove as if he were a beaver,' &c.

The pronunciation of the same word differs in different positions; thus, head will sometimes be hid, and sometimes hade.

'If so bein' is used instead of 'if' or 'if so be' of other dialects. 'Bein' is also used as 'since'. 'Being,' in this sense, may be found passim in the great work 'On the Creed', by Bishop Pearson, a native of Norfolk, first published in 1659.

A most remarkable elliptical use of the words *do, don't,* prevails; e.g., 'Has the postman called?' 'I don't know; *du* there's no letters for you.' 'Shet yin gate, Tim bor, *don't* them pigs 'll git out!'

These remarks are intended as supplemental to those of Forby, Moor, and others.

From the constant use of the Bible by all who can read just above the lower orders, our dialect has received a perceptible Biblical colouring; consequently, much difficulty has been experienced in setting forth a portion of Scripture in a dialect which differs less from Scripture than from any other work in correct English.

When the learned editor shall have completed the 'Promptorium Parvulorum' there will be more materials for the investigation of the Icenian than of any other English dialect from 1400 to the present time.

NOTE

Shortly after the First World War, whilst he was still serving as 'Captain of the Guard' at the Prisoner-of-War camp at West Tofts, the local historian and antiquary of King's Lynn, E. M. Beloe, had privately printed an edition of this work which he called the 'Greenland Fishery Museum Reprint'. As the 'Postscript' to this edition contains an explanation of how the 'Song' came to be translated into Norfolk dialect in the first place, it is printed here in full.

Postscript

I once saw a letter from the late Dean Goulburn stating that he would gladly give two guineas for a copy of the Norfolk 'Song of Solomon.' I would do so too, to add to my growing collection, but it seems that the book is entirely out of print; only two hundred and fifty copies were struck off; they were printed with the Song in twenty-three other English dialects at the expense of His Imperial Highness Prince Louis Lucien Bonaparte. I wish to express my thanks to Mr. R Colman, M.P., of Norwich, who has, without any hesitation, lent me the original, from which this reprint has been made. I have been able to attend to very little archæology during the War; but when on the subject of Norfolk dialect I should like to record that I have just bought at the Huth sale a copy of the 'Promptorium Parvulorum' compiled by the Black Friar and Anchorite of Lynn, Galfridus Grammaticus, and printed by Pynson in 1499. It can now be seen in the Greenland Fishery Museum.

E. M, B.

The Song of Solomon

from the 1611 Authorised Version of the Bible

CHAPTER I

The song of songs, which is Solomon's.

2. Let him kiss me with the kisses of his mouth: for thy love is better than wine.

3. Because of the savour of thy good ointments thy name is as ointment poured forth, therefore do the virgins love thee.

4. Draw me, we will run after thee: the king hath brought me into his chambers: we will be glad and rejoice in thee, we will remember thy love more than wine: the upright love thee.

5. I am black, but comely, O ye daughters of Jerusalem, as the tents of Kedar, as the curtains of Solomon.

6. Look not upon me, because I am black, because the sun hath looked upon me: my mother's children were angry with me; they made me the keeper of the vineyards; but mine own vineyard have I not kept.

7. Tell me, O thou whom my soul loveth, where thou feedest, where thou makest thy flock to rest at noon: for why should I be as one that turneth aside by the flocks of thy companions?

8. If thou know not, O thou fairest among women, go thy way forth by the footsteps of the flock, and feed thy kids beside the shepherd's tents.

9. I have compared thee, O my love, to a company of horses in Pharaoh's chariots.

The Song o' Sorlomun

translated into Norfolk dialect by Revd Edward Gillett.

CHAPTER 1.

The song o' songs, as is Sorlomun's.

2. Lerr 'in kiss me with the kisses of his mouth; for yar love is better 'an wine.

3. Becaze o' the smell o' yar good intements, yar name is as intements pored out, therefoor du the mawthers love yĕ.

4. Dror mĕ, we'll run arter yĕ: the king he ha' browt me into his charmbers: we'll be glad and rejice in ye; we'll remahmber yar love more 'an wine: the right-up love yĕ.

5. I em black, but tidy, O ye darters of J'rusal'm, as the taents o' Kedar, as the cattins o' Sorlomun.

6. Don't sin starrin at me, cos I em black, 'ecos the sun t' have barnt mĕ: my mother's children wor snāsty wi' me; they made me keeper o' the winyerds, but m' own winyerd I hā'nt kept.

7. Tell onto me, yow hu my soul du love, where ye fade, where ye make yar flock to rest at nune: fur why shud I be as one as tarn aside by yar cumrades' flock?

8. If so bein' as yĕ don't know, O yow bootifullest o' women, go yer ways furth by the futtin' of the flock, and feed yer kids 'eside the shepherds' tents.

9. I ha' likened yow, O my love, to a taamer o' hosses in Pharer's charrits.

10. Thy cheeks are comely with rows of jewels, thy neck with chains of gold.

11. We will make thee borders of gold with studs of silver.

12. While the king sitteth at his table, my spikenard sendeth forth the smell thereof.

13. A bundle of myrrh is my well-beloved unto me; he shall lie all night betwixt my breasts.

14. My beloved is unto me as a cluster of camphire in the vineyards of En-gedi.

15. Behold, thou art fair, my love; behold, thou art fair; thou hast doves' eyes.

16. Behold, thou art fair, my beloved, yea, pleasant: also our bed is green.

17. The beams of our house are cedar, and our rafters of fir.

CHAPTER 2

I am the rose of Sharon, and the lily of the valleys.

2. As the lily among thorns, so is my love among the daughters.

3. As the apple tree among the trees of the wood, so is my beloved among the sons. I sat down under his shadow with great delight, and his fruit was sweet to my taste.

4. He brought me to the banqueting house, and his banner over me was love.

5. Stay me with flagons, comfort me with apples: for I am sick of love.

10. Yar cheeks are right fine wi' 'ringes of jewiltry, yer neck wi' chanes o' gold.

11. We'll make for ye selvedges o' gold, wi' nubbles o' silver.

12. While the king he's a settin at his table, my spikenard du give out its smell.

13. A bundle o' myrrh is my well-beloved onto me; he shell lay all night atwin my brists.

14. My beloved is onto me as a bunch o' camphire i' the winyerds o' Engedi.

15. I sā! lookye, yow are feer, my love; you've got dows' eyes.

16. I sā! you are feer, my beloved; ah, and sweetful; likeways, our bed is green.

17. The summers o' our house are cedarn, and our balks o' deal.

CHAPTER 2.

The rose o' Shaaron I em, and the lily o' the walleys.

2. All the same as the lily amunst thorns, so is my love amunst the darters.

3. All the same as th' apple-tree amunst the trees o' the wud, so is my beloved amunst the sons. I set myself down ondernane his shadder wi' grate delight, and his fruit wor swate to my likin'.

4. He browt me to the faastin'-house, and his bander atop on me was love.

5. Stay me wi' gotches, comfort me wi' apples, for I em cothy wi' love.

6. His left hand is under my head, and his right hand doth embrace me.

7. I charge you, O ye daughters of Jerusalem, by the roes, and by the hinds of the field, that ye stir not up, nor awake my love, till he please.

8. The voice of my beloved! behold, he cometh leaping upon the mountains, skipping upon the hills.

9. My beloved is like a roe or a young hart: behold, he standeth behind our wall, he looketh forth at the windows, shewing himself through the lattice.

10. My beloved spake, and said unto me, Rise up, my love, my fair one, and come away.

11. For, lo, the winter is past, the rain is over and gone;

12. The flowers appear on the earth; the time of the singing of birds is come, and the voice of the turtle is heard in our land;

13. The fig tree putteth forth her green figs, and the vines with the tender grape give a good smell. Arise, my love, my fair one, and come away.

14. O my dove, that art in the clefts of the rock, in the secret places of the stairs, let me see thy countenance, let me hear thy voice; for sweet is thy voice, and thy countenance is comely.

15. Take us the foxes, the little foxes, that spoil the vines: for our vines have tender grapes.

16. My beloved is mine, and I am his: he feedeth among the lilies.

17. Until the day break, and the shadows flee away, turn, my beloved, and be thou like a roe or a young hart upon the mountains of Bether.

6. His left hand is ondernane my hid, and his right hand du cuddle me.

7. I charge yow, O ye darters o' J'rusal'm, b' the roes and b' the hinds o' the fild, that yow shawn't stir up, ner yit wake up my love till so bein' as he plaze.

8. The wīce o' my beloved! I sa! look how he du come a lopin' apun the mountins, a skippin' apun the hills.

9. My beloved, he is liken onto a roe or a young hart: look! how 'e stand behind our wall; he look out at our winders, a showin' hisself out at the casemint.

10. My beloved, he spook, and he sā onto me, Rise up my love, my feer un, and come awāh.

11. For, I sā; the winter t' be past, and the rain 'tis over and gorn.

12. The flowers they be sin apun the airth; the time of the bads singin is come, and the cuin o' the ringdow is heared in our land.

13. The fig-tree du putt out her green figs, an' the wine-trees wi' the tander grape give a good smell. Git up, my love, my feer un, and less come awāh.

14. O my dow, that's in the cricks of the rocks, in the secret places o' the stars, let me see yer countenance, let me hear yer wīce; for yar wīce t' be sweet, and yar countenance tidy.

15. Ketch us the foxes, the leetle foxes, as spile the wine-trees; for our wine ha' tander grapes.

16. My beloved is mine, and I em his; he du feed amunst the lilies.

17. Ontil the dā brake, and the shadders fly away, tarn, my beloved, be yow liken onto a roe or a young hart apun the mountins o' Bether.

CHAPTER 3

By night on bed I sought him whom my soul loveth: I sought him, but I found him not.

2. I will rise now, and go about the city in the streets, and in the broad ways I will seek him whom my soul loveth: I sought him, but I found him not.

3. The watchmen that go about the city found me: to whom I said, Saw ye him whom my soul loveth?

4. It was but a little that I passed from them, but I found him whom my soul loveth: I held him, and would not let him go, until I had brought him into my mother's house, and into the chamber of her that conceived me.

5. I charge you, O ye daughters of Jerusalem, by the roes, and by the hinds of the field, that ye stir not up, nor awake my love, till he please.

6. Who is this that cometh out of the wilderness like pillars of smoke, perfumed with myrrh and frankincense, with all powders of the merchant?

7. Behold his bed, which is Solomon's; threescore valiant men are about it, of the valiant of Israel.

8. They all hold swords, being expert in war: every man hath his sword upon his thigh because of fear in the night.

9. King Solomon made himself a chariot of the wood of Lebanon.

10. He made the pillars thereof of silver, the bottom thereof of gold, the covering of it of purple, the midst thereof being paved with love, for the daughters of Jerusalem.

11. Go forth, O ye daughters of Zion, and behold king Solomon with the crown wherewith his mother crowned him in the day of his espousals, and in the day of the gladness of his heart.

CHAPTER 3.

By night on my bed I hankered arter him hu my soul du love: I sarched arter 'im, but I fond him nut.

2. I'll get up now, and stroam about the city, in the lokes and canseys I'll seek him as my soul du love: I sarched arter 'im, but I fond him nut.

3. The watchmin that go about the city they fond me; and I said onto 'm, Ha' you sin him as my soul du love?

4. Jest a leetle arter I past from 'em, I fond him as my soul du love; I heu'd him, and wudn't ler 'im go, till I had browt him into my mother's house, and into the charmbers o' her as consaved me.

5. I charge ye, O yow darters of J'rusal'm, b' the roes and b' the hinds o' the fild, that ye don't stur up, nor yit wake up my love till so bein' as he plaze.

6. Who is this a comin' out o' the wildernese, like pillars o' roke, smellin' o' myrrh and frankincense, and all the powders o' the fogger?

7. Behold his bed, as is Sorlomun's: treescŏre dimmocks are about it, o' the waliant o' Isra'l.

8. They all hold swâds, bein' reglar dimmocks, every each man have his swâd on his thigh, in case o' fear i' the night.

9. King Sorlomun he made hisself a charret o' the wud of Lebanon.

10. He made the pillars tu't o' silver' the boke on't o' gold, the kiverin' on't o' pupple, the midst on't bein' paved wi' love for the darters o' J'rusal'm.

11. Go out, O ye darters o' Zion, and behold King Sorlomun, wi' the crownd as his mother crown'd him with in the dā when his sibrets wor out axed, and i' the dā o' the gladness o' his heart.

CHAPTER 4.

Behold, thou art fair, my love; behold, thou art fair; thou hast doves' eyes within thy locks: thy hair is as a flock of goats, that appear from mount Gilead.

2. Thy teeth are like a flock of sheep that are even shorn, which came up from the washing; whereof every one bear twins, and none is barren among them.

3. Thy lips are like a thread of scarlet, and thy speech is comely: thy temples are like a piece of a pomegranate within thy locks.

4. Thy neck is like the tower of David builded for an armoury, whereon there hang a thousand bucklers, all shields of mighty men.

5. Thy two breasts are like two young roes that are twins, which feed among the lilies.

6. Until the day break, and the shadows flee away, I will get me to the mountain of myrrh, and to the hill of frankincense.

7. Thou art all fair, my love; there is no spot in thee.

8. Come with me from Lebanon, my spouse, with me from Lebanon: look from the top of Amana, from the top of Shenir and Hermon, from the lions' dens, from the mountains of the leopards.

9. Thou hast ravished my heart, my sister, my spouse; thou hast ravished my heart with one of thine eyes, with one chain of thy neck.

10. How fair is thy love, my sister, my spouse! how much better is thy love than wine! and the smell of thine ointments than all spices!

CHAPTER 4.

I sā, look! yow're fair, my love; I sā, look! yow've dows' eyes 'ithin yar locks: yar hear is as a flock o' goots as appear from Mount Gilead.

2. Yar teeth air liken onto a flock o' ship jest clipt, as come up from th' washin'; and every one on 'em ha' tweens, and norn on 'em is gast.

3. Yar lips air liken onto a trid o' scarlet, and yar spache is sweetful; yar timples air liken onto a bit of pomegranate 'ithin yar locks.

4. Yar neck is liken onto the tower o' David built for an armowry, and onto 't there hang a thousen' bucklers, all shilds o' mighty min.

5. Yar tew titties air liken to tew young roes as air tweens, and feed amunst the lilies.

6. Till so bein' as the dā du brake, and the shadders fly awāh, I'll git me to the mountin o' myrrh, and the hill o' frankincense.

7. Yow're right on fair, my love; there ban't no spot in ye.

8. Come wi' me from the Lebanon, my missus, w' me from Lebanon; look down from atop of Amana, from atop o' Shenir and Hermon, from the lions' danes, and from the mountins o' lapuds.

9. Yow've took awāh m' heart, my suster, my missus; yow've took awāh m' heart wi' one o' yar eyes, wi' one chane o' yar neck.

10. Yar love, my suster, my missus, how fair t' be; how much better 'an wine is yar love, and the smell o' yar inteménts then all sorts o' spices!

11. Thy lips, O my spouse, drop as the honeycomb: honey and milk are under thy tongue; and the smell of thy garments is like the smell of Lebanon.

12. A garden inclosed is my sister, my spouse; a spring shut up, a fountain sealed.

13. Thy plants are an orchard of pomegranates, with pleasant fruits; camphire, with spikenard,

14. Spikenard and saffron; calamus and cinnamon, with all trees of frankincense; myrrh and aloes, with all the chief spices:

15. A fountain of gardens, a well of living waters, and streams from Lebanon.

16. Awake, O north wind; and come, thou south; blow upon my garden, that the spices thereof may flow out. Let my beloved come into his garden, and eat his pleasant fruits.

CHAPTER 5.

I am come into my garden, my sister, my spouse: I have gathered my myrrh with my spice; I have eaten my honeycomb with my honey; I have drunk my wine with my milk: eat, O friends; drink, yea, drink abundantly, O beloved.

2. I sleep, but my heart waketh: it is the voice of my beloved that knocketh, saying, Open to me, my sister, my love, my dove, my undefiled: for my head is filled with dew, and my locks with the drops of the night.

3. I have put off my coat; how shall I put it on? I have washed my feet; how shall I defile them?

4. My beloved put in his hand by the hole of the door, and my bowels were moved for him.

11. Yar lips, O my missus, they drope as the honeycomb; honey an' milk air ondernane yar tongue, and the smell o' yar duds is liken onto the smell o' Lebanon.

12. A yeard took in is my suster, my missus; a spring shet up, a fountin saled.

13. Yar plants, why they ba en orchard o' pomegranates, wi' plasant fruits; camphire wi' spikenard,

14. Spikenard and saffron, sweet seg and cinnamun, wi' all trees of frankincense; myrrh an' allers, wi' all of the hid spices.

15. A fountin o' yards, a well o' livin' waters, and becks from Lebanon.

16. Awake, O nor' wind; and come, yow south; blow into my yard, that its spices ma' flow out on it. Let my beloved come into 's yard and ate his plasant fruits.

CHAPTER 5.

I em come into my yard, my suster, my missus: I've got up my myrrh along wi' my spice; I've aten my honey-comb along wi' my honey; I ha' drunk my wine along wi' my milk: ate away, my frinds; ah! an' drink planty, O sweetheart.

2. I sleep, but my heart it's awake, ta be the wice o' my sweetheart, a knockin' sāin', Onsneck to me, my suster, my love, my dow, my ondefiled one! for my hid is filled wi' dew, and my locks wi' the dags o' the night.

3. I've put off my coot; how shull I pur it on? I ha' woished my fit; how shull I nasty 'em?

4. My beloved, he putt in his hand by the hole o' the door, and my innards wor moved for him.

5. I rose up to open to my beloved; my hands dropped with myrrh, and my fingers with sweet smelling myrrh, upon the handles of the lock.

6. I opened to my beloved; but my beloved had withdrawn himself, and was gone: my soul failed when he spake: I sought him, but I could not find him; I called him, but he gave me no answer.

7. The watchmen that went about the city found me, they smote me, they wounded me; the keepers of the walls took away my veil from me.

8. I charge you, O daughters of Jerusalem, if ye find my beloved, that ye tell him, that I am sick of love.

9. What is thy beloved more than another beloved, O thou fairest among women? what is thy beloved more than another beloved, that thou dost so charge us?

10. My beloved is white and ruddy, the chiefest among ten thousand.

11. His head is as the most fine gold, his locks are bushy, and black as a raven.

12. His eyes are as the eyes of doves by the rivers of waters, washed with milk, and fitly set.

13. His cheeks are as a bed of spices, as sweet flowers: his lips like lilies, dropping sweet smelling myrrh.

14. His hands are as gold rings set with the beryl: his belly is as bright ivory overlaid with sapphires.

15. His legs are as pillars of marble, set upon sockets of fine gold: his countenance is as Lebanon, excellent as the cedars.

16. His mouth is most sweet; yea, he is altogether lovely. This is my beloved, and this is my friend, O daughters of Jerusalem.

5. I riz up to onsneck for my beloved, and my hands droped myrrh, and my fingers sweet-smelling myrrh onto the sneck o' the lock.

6. I oped to my beloved, but my beloved he had took hisself off, and was gorn; my soul failed when he spook. I sowt 'im, but I cowdn't find 'im; I called 'im, but he answered norn.

7. The watchmen agoin' about the city fond me, they hit onto me, they wownded me; they as kept the walls, they took my wails from me.

8. Mind yow, O darters o' J'rusal'm, if so bein' yow luck to find my beloved, to tell onto him, that I fare cothy wi' love.

9. Wha's yar beloved more 'an 'nother beloved, yow feerest amunst women? Wha's yar beloved more 'an 'nother beloved, that yĕ tell us to mind so?

10. My beloved is white and rosy, the master one amunst tane thousan'.

11. His hid is most gay gold; his locks air bushy, an' black as a raven.

12. His eyes air liken onto dows' eyes by the strames o' water, woished wi' milk, and right properly set.

13. His cheeks air liken onto a bed o' spices, as sweet flowers: his lips liken onto lilies, a dropin' wi' sweet smellin myrrh.

14. His hands air as gowlden rings set wi' the beryl: his balely as bright ivory all done over wi' sapphires.

15. His legs air as postesses o' marble, set apun tennonts o' gay gowld: his countenance as Lebanon excellent as the cedars.

16. His mouth is stammin' sweet; ah, he's right on lovely. This here be my beloved, and this here be my friend, O ye darters o' J'rusal'm.

CHAPTER 6.

Whither is thy beloved gone, O thou fairest among women? whither is thy beloved turned aside? that we may seek him with thee.

2. My beloved is gone down into his garden, to the beds of spices, to feed in the gardens, and to gather lilies.

3. I am my beloved's, and my beloved is mine: he feedeth among the lilies.

4. Thou art beautiful, O my love, as Tirzah, comely as Jerusalem, terrible as an army with banners.

5. Turn away thine eyes from me, for they have overcome me: thy hair is as a flock of goats that appear from Gilead.

6. Thy teeth are as a flock of sheep which go up from the washing, whereof every one beareth twins, and there is not one barren among them.

7. As a piece of a pomegranate are thy temples within thy locks.

8. There are threescore queens, and fourscore concubines, and virgins without number.

9. My dove, my undefiled is but one; she is the only one of her mother, she is the choice one of her that bare her. The daughters saw her, and blessed her; yea, the queens and the concubines, and they praised her.

10. Who is she that looketh forth as the morning, fair as the moon, clear as the sun, and terrible as an army with banners?

11. I went down into the garden of nuts to see the fruits of the valley, and to see whether the vine flourished, and the pomegranates budded.

CHAPTER 6.

What way-wards is yar beloved gorn, O yow feerest amunst women? What way-wards is yar beloved tarned o' one side, that we may sarch arter 'im wi' yĕ?

2. My beloved, he is gorn down into 's yard, to the beds o' spices, and to feed in the yards, and to gather lilies.

3. I em my beloved's, and my beloved he is mine: he du feed amunst the lilies.

4. Yow air bootiful, O my love, as Tirzah, tidy as J'rusal'm, frightful as a army wi' banders.

5. Tarn awāh yar eyes from off o' mĕ, for they ha' bate mĕ: yar hear is as a flock o' goots as appear from Gilead.

6. Yar teeth air as a flock o' ship agoin' up from woishin', and every one on 'em bear tweens, and there a'n't norn gast amunst 'em.

7. Liken onto a bit o' pomegranate air yar tameples wuthin yar locks.

8. There be treescŏre queens, and fourscŏre concubines, and an onendless number o' maidens.

9. My dow, my ondefiled, is but one; she's the solintāry one of her mother; she's the chīce un o' her as had her. The darters saw her, an' blessed her; the queens, ah, an' the concubines, and they praised her.

10. Who's she as star out as the mornin', feer as the mune, shear as the sun, and frightful as an army wi' banders?

11. I went down into the nutsherd to look over the fruits o' the walley, to see wuther the wine-trees moised, and the pomegranates blŏwed.

12. Or ever I was aware, my soul made me like the chariots of Amminadib.

13. Return, return, O Shulamite; return, return, that we may look upon thee. What will ye see in the Shulamite? As it were the company of two armies.

CHAPTER 7.

How beautiful are thy feet with shoes, O prince's daughter! the joints of thy thighs are like jewels, the work of the hands of a cunning workman.

2. Thy navel is like a round goblet, which wanteth not liquor: thy belly is like an heap of wheat set about with lilies.

3. Thy two breasts are like two young roes that are twins.

4. Thy neck is as a tower of ivory; thine eyes like the fishpools in Heshbon, by the gate of Bath-rabbim: thy nose is as the tower of Lebanon which looketh toward Damascus.

5. Thine head upon thee is like Carmel, and the hair of thine head like purple; the king is held in the galleries.

6. How fair and how pleasant art thou, O love, for delights!

7. This thy stature is like to a palm tree, and thy breasts to clusters of grapes.

8. I said, I will go up to the palm tree, I will take hold of the boughs thereof: now also thy breasts shall be as clusters of the vine, and the smell of thy nose like apples;

9. And the roof of thy mouth like the best wine for my beloved, that goeth down sweetly, causing the lips of those that are asleep to speak.

10. I am my beloved's, and his desire is toward me.

12. Afore I was awores on't, my soul made me liken onto the charrets of Amminadib.

13. Tarn back! tarn back! O Shulamite! tarn back! tarn back! that we may look apun ye! What will ye see in the Shulamite? Suffin liken to the cumpany o' tew armies.

CHAPTER 7.

How pritty air yar feet wi' shues, O prince's darter! the jints o' yar thighs are like jewiltry, the handiwork of a knowin' workman.

2. Yar noble is like onto a round beaker as don't want no licker; yar baally like onto a hape of whate set about wi' lilies.

3. Yar tew titties air liken to tew young roes as air tweens.

4. Yar neck is an ivory steeple; yar eyes liken to the fishponds in Heshbon, by the gate o' Bethrabin; yar nose as the steeple o' Lebanon lookin' Damascus-wards.

5. Yar hid on ye is liken onto Carmel, and the hear o' yar hid like pupple: the king he's hew'd in the galleries.

6. How fair and how pleasant yow be for delights, O love.

7. This your hayt is liken onto a palmentree, and yar brists to a bunch o' grapes.

8. I sed I'll go right up onto the palmentree; I'll lay hold of its boughs; now also yar brists shall be as bunches o' from off the wine-tree, and the smell o' yar nostrils like apples.

9. And the ruff o' yar mouth liken onto the best wine for my beloved, as go down sweetfully, makin' the lips o' them as air asleep to spake.

10. I am my dare's, and his longin' is to me-wards.

11. Come, my beloved, let us go forth into the field; let us lodge in the villages.

12. Let us get up early to the vineyards; let us see if the vine flourish, whether the tender grape appear, and the pomegranates bud forth: there will I give thee my loves.

13. The mandrakes give a smell, and at our gates are all manner of pleasant fruits, new and old, which I have laid up for thee, O my beloved.

CHAPTER 8.

O that thou wert as my brother, that sucked the breasts of my mother! when I should find thee without, I would kiss thee; yea, I should not be despised.

2. I would lead thee, and bring thee into my mother's house, who would instruct me: I would cause thee to drink of spiced wine of the juice of my pomegranate.

3. His left hand should be under my head, and his right hand should embrace me.

4. I charge you, O daughters of Jerusalem, that ye stir not up, nor awake my love, until he please.

5. Who is this that cometh up from the wilderness, leaning upon her beloved? I raised thee up under the apple tree: there thy mother brought thee forth: there she brought thee forth that bare thee.

6. Set me as a seal upon thine heart, as a seal upon thine arm: for love is strong as death; jealousy is cruel as the grave: the coals thereof are coals of fire, which hath a most vehement flame.

11. Come, my dare, le's go out into the fild, le's lodge in the willages.

12. Le's gir up airly to the winyerds; le's see if the wine-tree be a moisin'; wuther the tander grapes come, and the pomegranate blŏw: there, my beloved, I'll gi' ye my loves.

13. The mandrakes they give a smell, and again our gates are all mander o' pleasant fruits, new and old, which I've laid up for my beloved!

CHAPTER 8.

How I du wish you wor liken onto my brather, as sucked the titties o' my mother! if so bein' I shu'd fond you out o' doors, I'd kiss ye; ah! I shudn't be looked down on.

2. I'd lade yow, and bring yow inter my mother's house, and she'd larn mĕ: I'd make yow drink o' the spiced wine o' the juice o' my pomegranate.

3. His left hand shu'd be ondernane my hid, and his right hand shu'd cuddle me.

4. Mind yow don't stir up, O darters o' J'rusal'm, n' yit wake up my beloved ontil so be as he plaze.

5. Who is this here a-comin' up from the heerth, a-lanin' on her beloved? I riz ye up ondernane the apple-tree; there yar mother browt ye foorth; there she browt ye foorth as had yĕ.

6. Set me as a sale apun yar heart; as a sale apun yar arm; for love is as strong as deerth; jallusy's as cruel as the grave; the coals on it air coals o' fire, as ha' got a right-on stammin' flame.

7. Many waters cannot quench love, neither can the floods drown it: if a man would give all the substance of his house for love, it would utterly be contemned.

8. We have a little sister, and she hath no breasts: what shall we do for our sister in the day when she shall be spoken for?

9. If she be a wall, we will build upon her a palace of silver: and if she be a door, we will inclose her with boards of cedar.

10. I am a wall, and my breasts like towers: then was I in his eyes as one that found favour.

11. Solomon had a vineyard at Baal-hamon; he let out the vineyard unto keepers; every one for the fruit thereof was to bring a thousand pieces of silver.

12. My vineyard, which is mine, is before me: thou, O Solomon, must have a thousand, and those that keep the fruit thereof two hundred.

13. Thou that dwellest in the gardens, the companions hearken to thy voice: cause me to hear it.

14. Make haste, my beloved, and be thou like to a roe or to a young hart upon the mountains of spices.

7. Lots o' water can't squench love, nayther can't the fluds drownd it; if so bein' a man had gan all his houseful for love, 'twu'd be right made nowt on.

8. We've a leetle suster, and she ha'n't got no brists; wha' shell we du for our suster in the day when she shell be axed for?

9. If so bein she's a wall, we'll build apun 'er a palast o' silver; an' if she's a door, we'll kiver her in with cedarn boards.

10. I em a wall, an' my brists all the same as steeples: then I wor in his eyes as one that fond favour.

11. Sorlomun he'd a winyerd at Baalhamon: he ler' out the winyerd unto keepers, everyone for the fruit on it wor to bring a thousand kines o' silver.

12. My winyerd, as is mine, is in frunt o' me: yow, O Sorlomun, must ha' a thousan'; an' them as keep the fruit on it tew hundred.

13. I sā! yow that live in the gardens, the cumrades listen t' yar wīce: make me for to heer it.

14. I sā! be brisk, now, my beloved, and be yow liken onto a roe or a young hart on the mountins o' spices.